Creative Christmas
Coloring Book

Marjorie Sarnat

Dover Publications, Inc.
Mineola, New York

Christmas joy abounds in this delightful coloring book! More than thirty beautifully drawn scenes depict seasonal images of stockings filled with adorable animals, characters from *The Nutcracker*, toys, a variety of angels, a pair of cute kittens in mittens, and a festive gingerbread house. Other heartwarming holiday pictures include Christmas villages, carolers, and, of course—Santa Claus! Intricate borders of poinsettia leaves, ornaments, ringing bells, and other decorative designs adorn the pages as well. Just select your media and experiment with the colors of your choice as you enjoy the artistic possibilities of this special collection—plus, the perforated, unbacked pages make displaying your work easy!

Bibliographical Note

Creative Christmas Coloring Book is a new work, first published
by Dover Publications, Inc., in 2018.

International Standard Book Number

ISBN-13: 978-0-486-82779-7
ISBN-10: 0-486-82779-8

Manufactured in the United States by LSC Communications
82779802   2018
www.doverpublications.com